FIREFLY LAMP

AISHI

Copyright © Aishi
All Rights Reserved.

This book has been published with all efforts taken to make the material error-free after the consent of the author. However, the author and the publisher do not assume and hereby disclaim any liability to any party for any loss, damage, or disruption caused by errors or omissions, whether such errors or omissions result from negligence, accident, or any other cause.

While every effort has been made to avoid any mistake or omission, this publication is being sold on the condition and understanding that neither the author nor the publishers or printers would be liable in any manner to any person by reason of any mistake or omission in this publication or for any action taken or omitted to be taken or advice rendered or accepted on the basis of this work. For any defect in printing or binding the publishers will be liable only to replace the defective copy by another copy of this work then available.

MOS

showing the path

to my fireflies.

Contents

Contents

Contents

Contents

Contents

Contents

Foreword

to the readers

i know
you feel
lost and confused
sometimes
about what has
happened
to us.
Sit
read
think
then
act.

Preface

why?
a 17 year old
teenager
student
daughter
sister
friend
lover
goal seeker
global citizen
should think like this...

Acknowledgements

nature

with love

Maa, Bapi,Bhai

for being the

base

on which

I

stand

Growl

They don't have words.

Yet, they speak.

1. 1

There she comes,
with her usual joy
and unusual calm eyes.
Pink lolled out tongue
dripping dry drools.
She doesn't complain.
About,
Skeletal pockmarked body,
Uprooted rough fur,
Persistent wagging tail.
Her six naked nipples,
One for each child.
First, the black
Crushed under a truck.
Second, the brown
stillborn and decomposed.
Third, the artistic
Gagged to death.
Fourth, mom's beloved
skeletal but playful.
Fifth, the unknown father's type
Sucked by teaks.
Last but not the least

Running behind mommy,
the most beautiful, indeed.

2. 2

How savoring!
The wingless,
Caged parrot.
Is fed with chillis,
to speak
and add spice
in her master's life.

3. 3

I was a starving mother,
Looking for some food,
You fed me bullets
for your good.
My child died.
Just for my hunger?
Or eating your food,
Was my a grave blunder?

4. 4

Life is a right.
Not a given privilege.
Then, why are we killed?
To devour human rage?

5. 5

You take your child
to the caged zoo,
still, humanity toward us
Is always booed.
Our pitiful condition
Never swoons you,
Our destruction
Always entertains you.

6. 6

I was born like this.
Cracked open
from a blissful egg.
A bifurcated baby tongue.
Slithering out
in the moist soil.
As sleek as a tendril.
As soft as fur.
I was guiltless.
Nature painted me
colorful.
God gifted me
hissing.
The man claimed me,
Unholy.
Cut me into half
because
I was a serpent.

7.7

You slit our throats.
Peel our skins.
Your branded leather bag
Piles up your sins.

8. 8

No matter
what my
breed, cost,
origin is
I do miss
my mother.
I might be
sold out,
bought,
breed
and fed
My bond with her
will never break.

9.9

Deeper than
the ocean
thicker than
the water
I licked
and cleaned
your gifted wounds
In less than a quarter.
Next time
when you'll visit
please ignore me and
pass by.
Those stones
aren't for
shooting and amusement.

10. 10

Nature is a pawn
being sold in the market
line up for buying Her,
With the money
in your pocket.
Hunters have the victory
murderers claim the throne,
poachers play the game
wildlife is left
to perish alone.

Eutopia

11. 11

Those costly medicines
Won't extend the longevity
increase productivity
or bring prosperity.
If you want
to push morbidity
then decant your blackbile
and sediment your personality.

12. 12

It is interesting to note
That the
lust parasite,
Require two hosts.
Body and mind,
to complete
The life cycle.
The female body
is a potential
trigger, too.

13. 13

The skin on our body,

the main barrier,

prevents the entry of criticism.

Consistency,

Coat chest and head.

Trap ill habits

from entering.

The acid in the stomach,

Words in the mouth,

tears from eyes

all constrict the antagonist's growth.

14. 14

Egos
are pathogenic.
They enter the host,
through society.
Multiply and interfere
with natural bonds.
Result in
Qualitative degrade
of character.

15. 15

Humans are good at imagination.
from
Invisible land barriers,
Cracked reputations,
Crumbling relations,
To
poisoned love
and
backstabbing respect.
All are fictions
to conceal
Flickering human mind.

16. 16

God and nature,
in unison.
Please gift a lake
the mirror of humanity.
So that
your narcissist child
could see
the in-between
of his rights and greed.

17. 17

Healthy hearts become cancerous
induced by sins.
Each oncogenic piece
possesses genes
the social carcinogens
accumulate like a mass
proliferating infected individuals
Malignancy of the world.
Invade and damage rapidly
transforming the rest
to its kind.
Alas! there is no cure.
but early detection is viable.
Help and sympathize them,
Instead of being shunned.
A problem to be dealt
hand in hand.
A malady to be tackled
With love and mercy
acting together.

18. 18

Our core
is not a prison.
To put lovers
behind bars.
They will simply
Break out.
Leaving
A thousand scars.
It's not a land
to be won
Over a fight.
You will hurt yourself
with a
stabbing knife.

19. 19

How beautiful
It would have been,
To differentiate
delta amount of
happiness
from the
infinitely long
dull sheet of life
and integrate it
to positive infinity.

20. 20

Not knowing
is not a fault.
But
pretending not
to know
is a crime.
Those pair of
Ignorant eyes
looks more
dingy
then a dark cave.

Teen

21. 21

I miss,
The kindergarten days.
So simple and innocent.
Not being,
Stared at
for wiping a boy's tears.
Questioned about
my skirt's length.
Commented on
holding hands.
Enquired upon
receiving a rose.

22. 22

Thoughts come to me
Like streaming water.
to let my
patch of words
evolve in
a diverse forest of
poetry.

23. 23

Do you
feel that void?
In the body center.
No matter
How much
You are packed
With family and friends.
That octahedron's limb
will connect
the faces of
your unsolved cube.

24. 24

How does it
feel to be wasted?
You have
everything;
But you don't know
How to utilize
anything.

25. 25

Stars don't judge
neither clip the wings
they know how to fly
breaking all the strings
just speak out about everything
till you are done
take a deep breath
your pain will be gone.

26. 26

Surely,
metamorphosis
is a massacre
when a child
transforms
and flies away
in front of
parents' eyes.

27. 27

Acne appears
before makeup.
To remind me
to correct
rather conceal
my flaws.

28. 28

Each one of us
is solenoid.
Hollow cylinder
knowingly
wrapped with wire
of insecurities
doubts and jealousy.
More the number
of loops
more the pain
and suffering.

29. 29

It's natural
to overlook
parent's sacrifice
facilities
grades
relations
goals
expectations
while dipping
in a shallow pool of
fantasy.
You won't understand
until thrown in the ocean.

30. 30

we all
go through this phase
confused
with the path.
My firefly lamp
will help you
ahead.

she,her

31. 31

The moon,
waits for her sisters
to walk freely
at midnight
on the city roads
to admire the beauty.

32. 32

Not everyone
is daddy's princess.
Some were the family's
burden.
They became
the aborted defects.

33. 33

You gifted me roses
stolen from a garden
we went on a drive
run by father's sweat
we dined with luxury
deprived of mother's meal
you proposed to me
with wet lips,
are you masculine?
without honesty.
A true man
is the one
who touches
woman's heart
not her breast.

34. 34

Castrate
the rapists
so that
they could feel
the pinning pain
of high pitched
screams.

35. 35

she
fed you
the colostrum
to provide you
antibodies
so that
you don't become
antigens
to other people.

36. 36

Mothers,
please become
the weedicide
if your planted
seed
turns out
to be a weed.

37. 37

she
never pleaded
to bleed
freely
in the
bleak world.

38. 38

Why
does his
pupils
droop down
when
he sees her.
Is it lust
or shame?

39. 39

She is
biologically superior
physically durable
heartily safe.
But
socially inferior
emotionally unstable
sexually vulnerable.
Others are waiting
to balance
her talents
with antagonistic weights.

40. 40

what a seen of
still eyes,
wider than the
wings that fly.
she remained
tattered and scattered
alone
on the roadside...

bullets

41. 41

Soldiers
march to the battlefield
with their handsome faces.
Return home
after victory
boxed up
as unidentifiable pieces.

42. 42

Three letters in a tussle
disguised but true brothers
envy at their metal hearts
ddivided their solitary mother.

43. 43

What if
all the flags of countries
blended with
earth's colors.
We could see
the prettiest
smiles on their faces.

44. 44

When wars
begin
Thousands slaughter
each other.
Rivers of blood flow.
A girl loses
her father.

45. 45

what was
the world war
fashion?
Skinny skeletons
toes-less legs
fallen teeth
lidless eyes
blood lipstick.

46. 46

when
identical twins
fight over
one placenta
the mother
has to
forcefully
expel
both of them
out
of her womb.

47. 47

Peeling off
hanging skin.
blasting
the blisters.
Breathing
in smog.
Becoming
an amputee.
Watching
sky fall.
Is common
during
air raid.

48. 48

Can
barbed wire
separate
soil grains?

49. 49

Is'nt it painful
to see
your brother
shot down
by your other
brother
amidst
the boundaries.

50. 50

I
can't
stop you
from fighting wars.
But
I can
prick
your conscience
as deep as a
bullet
prior to
the next war.

dual nature

51. 51

Tress produces sperms
fruits are ripened ovaries,
flower
is the holiest symbol
of sexuality.
Every process is pure
till our
thoughts
pollute it.

52. 52

The wall
on which he
urinates
doesn't care.
The people who talk
behind his back
when he rains,
are doubtful
of his manners.

53. 53

You are beloved
till
your income
exceeds
your
input.

54. 54

How is
metropolitan life?
The sky is gray
buildings are blue.
Tress are black
papers are green.
Emotions are hidden
behind
formal crooked smile.

55. 55

Let our

tongues

run a marathon.

Where its important

to be

fully expressed

not

to be

the first

to express.

56. 56

Normal parents
are stretched
in a tug of war
between
clock and currency.

57. 57

You won't
understand the
meaning of
"home sweet home"
till
you only get to visit
your house
on vacations.

58. 58

Social media
is a majestic
dollhouse.
Everything is
plastic and plastered.

59. 59

I wish
the tress
could shout.
The world
would have been
healthier.

60. 60

Hunger
is the absence of food?
close your eyes
and feel.
The acid in the stomach
feeds on the walls.
Dry cracked mouth
chocked with
eroded teeth.
Every inch
of the skin
pinned to the ground.
A vulture
waiting
to feed on your
corpse.

penniless

61. 61

Poverty
dances with the
dark.
To the music of
empty tin cans
growling stomachs
and low pitched screams.

62. 62

People are
mentally
bankrupt.
The tend to
rob
feelings.

63. 63

Poverty
increases
when
hugs
reduces
to
formal
smiles.

64. 64

You are rich
only
when
your relations
exceed
the number of notes
you have.

65. 65

What
is more
excruciating?
Pain of hunger
or
pain of death?

66. 66

Beggars
are those
who beg
for mercy
and
carry
forward it
to next the
generation.

67. 67

Diamonds
are
overpriced
allotropes
of carbon.
Graphite
is
priceless
tool
of creativity.
The origin
is the same.

68. 68

Refract
the humans
through a prism
and see
diverse
bands of characters.
Pilled up
one above the other
like
immiscible
layers of oil.
How will
literacy
filter out?

69. 69

How does currency
become green?
It drained
out the greenery
from the forests.

70. 70

are we
immune?
to ouselves,
to greed and
gluttony?

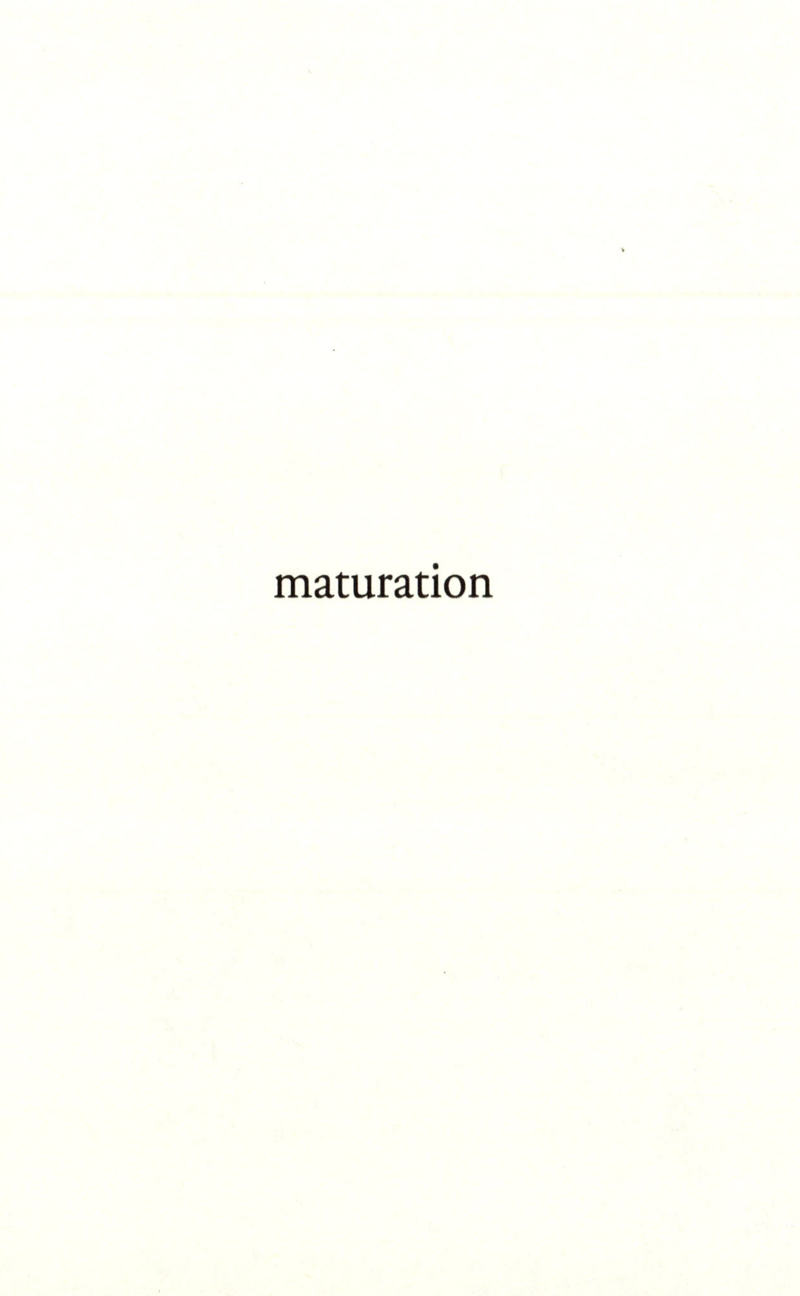

maturation

71. 71

Did the monster
under my bed
grow old?
or
the child
inside me
grew up?

72. 72

we have searched for
heaven and hell in
all wrong places
it's in us
it's us.

73. 73

you
shift people
aside
to reach
your
destiny.
Don't forget
to
donate
atleast
a penny.

74. 74

75. 75

My childhood was
most beautiful.
My heart
was my own music
not a division
of
atrium and ventricle.

76. 76

Chemistry,
was there
the bond between us
we never cared
love is an excess of
oxytocin.

77.77

That time
the rainbow
in the sky
were colors in flight.
Not
Huygens's principle
of dispersion
of light.

78. 78

Black clouds
of maturity
rained
and settled
the suspended
particles
of my curiocity.

79. 79

Love
can
sew
time's
wounds.

80. 80

Maturity
dies
when
you
become
dependent.

entropy

measure

of

randomness.

81. 81

silence
and peace
are the
two whorls
of the
same flower.

82. 82

the more
you smoke
the faster
you reduce
the surface area
of your
life.

83. 83

he
cried aloud
in front of
you
because
he knew.
"you are worth it"

84. 84

man's tears
are dewdrops
appear
at the sunless dawn
and moonless dusk.

85. 85

who will
light the candles?
when
humanity
will rest in peace.

86. 86

Cheaters
are ripened
by growing
betrayal's fungus.
It gives them
a devastating flavor.

87. 87

Can
antibiotics
cure
our
mental
leprosy?

88. 88

Puffed up
appearance
of fake people's
chest
is due
to
accumulation
of exhaled
poison gas.

89. 89

the
color
white
is
not
blank.
It
cleverly
expresses
itself.

90. 90

I
want
to
scuba dive
a camera
into my heart
and click
pictures
of its
laccrerated walls.

91. 91

Mirror mirror
on the wall
which is
the safest
place
in the
world?

92. 92

you feel
so lonely
still
not being
alone
you do
have relations
with
people
made of
stones.

93. 93

94. 94

stars
were the people
unaffected
by avarice
they are
specially appointed
to listen
to
your cries.

95. 95

Come
look at the horizon
where land and sea
meets
two lovers
lost in each other
and
a widow weeps.

96. 96

Every
jingle
of her anklets
had an
echo
in his heart.
The thread
that connects them
never
lets them
fall apart.

97. 97

The pitter-patter
on the roof
with the breezes
from the Nile.
Calms the mind
and soothes the veins
its so nice
to be a pluviophile.

98. 98

Each and every
moment
that we spent
all of a sudden
it came to an end.
Where no more
I can feel you
my only lovebird
flew.
Broke the cage
of my heart
never be put back
together.
Feeling of your absense
is endless
my life
has become
meaningless.
Your lifeless body
lies in my front
every memory of yours
haunts.
Only thing left

is your
Grave.

99. 99

I
am dressed
all in black
with your picture
in front.
Hunting for a rhythm
of your heartbeat
The only thing I get
is defeat.
I am left
to sob in the darkness
deprived of you
love, care, and kindness.
Tears roll down my cheeks
My emptiness makes
me weep.
But
I promise
to stand up again
because
you will look
down from
heaven.

I have your last wish
to fulfill
before that
I won't fall ill.

100. 100

They look into their eyes
in the twilight of the moon
Pure love
was born
from the troth
of boon and doom.
The creator of the earth
accompanied by the devastator
together connected the bond
of heaven and hell
for forever.

your own space

express

yourself.

101..

102. ..

103. ...

104. ....

105. .....

bonus

the

extra

edge

you

achive

over

yourself

becomes

the bonus

competition

to

others.

why you?

you are shielded

your

heart

is

shielded

dorsally

ventrally

latterly.

do you feel safe?

continue

only

few

can

continue

forward

after

looking

back.

can you?

roots

the

deeper

your

roots

penetrate

the

stronger

you stand.

do you?

oxytosin

does

love

has

something

beyond

oxytocin?

is it true?

Firefly Lamp

MOS

Finally
I have made
my
firefly lamp
it
won't be
dark
anymore

www.ingramcontent.com/pod-product-compliance
Lightning Source LLC
Chambersburg PA
CBHW061343160726
47995CB00001B/147